W9-BMV-195

MOUNT ST. HELENS NATIONAL VOLCANIC MONUMENT

A TRUE BOOK

by

Sharlene and Ted Nelson

Children's Press®
A Division of Grolier Publishing
New York London Hong Kong Sydney
Danbury, Connecticut

Reading Consultant
Linda Cornwell
Learning Resource Consultant
Indiana Department
of Education

Subject Consultant
Jim Quiring
Director Coldwater Ridge
Visitor Center
Mount St. Helens National
Volcanic Monument

Library of Congress Cataloging-in-Publication Data

Nelson, Sharlene P.
Mount St. Helens National Volcanic Monument / by Sharlene Nelson and Ted Nelson.
p. cm. —(A True book)
Includes bibliographical references and index.
Summary: Describes the destruction caused by the eruption of Mount St. Helens in 1980, the slow return of plant and animal life, and the special area set aside to study this renewal.
ISBN: 0-516-20444-0 (lib. bdg.) 0-516-26269-6 (pbk.)
1. Natural history—Washington (State)—Mount Saint Helens National Volcanic Monument—Juvenile literature. 2. Ecology—Washington (State)—Mount Saint Helens National Volcanic Monument—Juvenile literature. 3. Mount Saint Helens National Volcanic Monument (Wash.)—Juvenile literature. 4. Saint Helens, Mount (Wash.)—Eruption, 1980—Environmental aspects—Juvenile literature. [1. Mount Saint Helens National Volcanic Monument (Wash.) 2. Ecology—Washington (State) 3. Saint Helens, Mount (Wash.)—Eruption, 1980. 4. Volcanoes.]
I. Nelson, Ted W. II. Title. III. Series.
QH105.W2N44 1997
508.797'84—dc21 96-46738CIP
AC

Printed in the United States of America.
1 2 3 4 5 6 7 8 9 10 R 06 05 04 03 02 01 00 99 98 97

Contents

WASHINGTON
CANADA
Puget Sound
WASHINGTON
IDAHO
Seattle
Spokane
Tacoma
Olympia
PACIFIC OCEAN
Area of Detail
Mount St. Helens National Volcanic Monument
Columbia River
N
W
E
S
OREGON
MOUNT ST. HELENS NATIONAL VOLCANIC MONUMENT
Spirit Lake
Mount St. Helens
0
200 miles
0
300 kilometers
0
5 miles
0
7 kilometers

Why Make a Volcanic Monument?

Do you know what a volcanic eruption is? A volcano is a mountain with openings, called vents. When a volcano erupts, hot gases, rocks, ash, and lava can be thrown out of its vents. A volcanic eruption can destroy much of the land, wildlife, and plants that surround the volcano. Can you imagine how long it might take for the plants and animals to return to an area after a volcano erupts? Well, neither could the scientists who study volcanoes. But on May 18, 1980, a volcano in southwest Washington called Mount St. Helens erupted. Now, scientists have a place to study how nature renews itself after a volcano erupts. It is called

A scientist uses special equipment to track animals in the monument.

Mount St. Helens National Volcanic Monument. You can go there and see for yourself.

Mount St. Helens National Volcanic Monument is 110,000 acres (44,500 hectares), about twice the size of Washington,

D.C. The monument includes Mount St. Helens and much of the area that was destroyed by the 1980 eruption. The United States Congress established the monument in 1982.

Before Mount St. Helens erupted, it was a beautiful mountain that stood 9,677 feet (2,950 meters) high. Its snow-covered sides sloped down to a thick forest. At the mountain's northern base lay Spirit Lake. Snow-fed rivers

Mount St. Helens and Spirit Lake before the eruption

flowed through the forest. In the summer, campers fished in the lake and hiked along tree-lined trails.

The Mountain Erupts

At 8:32 A.M. on May 18, 1980, Mount St. Helens erupted. A powerful earthquake beneath the mountain caused a landslide. Masses of snow, ice, and rock slid down one side of the mountain. The landslide, called an avalanche, was the largest in history.

As Mount St. Helens erupted, the white snow on the mountain was covered by gray ash.

When the eruption was over, about 1,300 feet (396 m) of the mountain was gone, and Spirit Lake was covered with fallen trees.

Part of the avalanche fell into Spirit Lake. It caused a huge wave to wash up from the lake onto the surrounding hills. The wave toppled giant trees. As the wave fell back into the lake, it carried many of the fallen trees with it.

Another part of the avalanche plunged 14 miles (23 kilometers) down a river valley. In some places, the rocks, ash, and chunks of ice were 600 feet (183 m) deep.

Meanwhile, a blast of ash and hot gases zoomed away from the mountain like a rocket. Near the mountain, the blast traveled at about

650 miles (1,046 km) per hour. The gases were heated to 550 degrees Fahrenheit (288 degrees Celsius)—hot enough to melt a tin can.

On the mountainsides, snow and ice that had been melted by the hot gases mixed with ash and formed a giant mass of mud. The mud flowed down the mountain and into the rivers that led away from the mountain.

A dark cloud of ash rose 16 miles (26 km) into the sky

The huge ash cloud that rose from the volcano traveled for hundreds of miles.

above the mountain. Part of the cloud was carried away by winds. It traveled east toward Montana and north into Canada.

After the Eruption

Soon after Mount St. Helens erupted, scientists began to explore the area they called the "blast zone." The scientists found a huge hole, or crater, in the mountain. Almost 1,300 feet (396 m) of the mountaintop had been blown away by the blast. The blast

The top photograph shows Mount St. Helens and the surrounding area (including Spirit Lake) before the eruption. The bottom photograph shows the same area after the eruption. Note that all of the trees and grass are gone, hills are flattened, and most of the mountaintop is blown off.

zone was enormous. It covered an area of about 150,000 acres (61,000 ha). The land was covered with gray ash. Steam from melting chunks of ice rose above the rocks and ash.

On the surrounding hills, trees as tall as 200 feet (61 m) had been broken into millions of tiny, sharp pieces. Other trees, blown down by the volcano's blast, laid like matchsticks in the ash. The entire area was very quiet. There were no birds to sing or insects to

Dead trees littered the ground in the blast zone.

buzz. When Mount St. Helens erupted, 200 bears, 5,000 deer, and 1,500 elk were killed. Fifty-seven people who were near the volcano were also killed. It looked like all of the life in the blast zone had been destroyed.

Harry R. Truman

Harry R. Truman was eighty-three years old in 1980. He lived in a lodge at Spirit Lake. In March 1980, scientists thought that Mount St. Helens would erupt soon. The area was dangerous. People who lived in the area left. But Harry refused to leave his home.

For two months, Harry was interviewed on television. Schoolchildren wrote letters to Harry asking him to leave his lodge so he would be safe.

One Saturday some friends visited Harry. They hoped to convince him to leave. But Harry said, "No."

The next morning Mount St. Helens erupted. Harry and his lodge were buried under the rocks and ash. Harry's death was sad, but many people still remember him.

During the months after the eruption, scientists began to find survivors. In the surrounding mountains, the snow had sheltered many of the trees and huckleberry bushes. This snow shelter protected the trees and bushes from the direct path of the blast.

Thick layers of ice that covered lakes high in the mountains had protected the fish and frogs underwater. Insect nests that were

Insects, including grasshoppers, survived the eruption because their nests were safe underground.

underground or were inside decaying (rotting) logs had survived too. And mice, moles, and gophers began to poke their noses through the ash. They had been safe in their underground burrows.

Colors Return

At first, no plants could grow in the ash. But soon the moles and gophers became the blast zone's gardeners. Their underground tunneling mixed ash from above the ground with rich soil from below. This helped to make tiny holes for seeds that were

Scientists thought that nothing could grow in the deep ash that covered the blast zone (top). As gophers began to tunnel beneath the ground again (left), they helped to make the soil rich so plants could grow.

blown in on the wind. The seeds landed in the holes and began to grow.

Fireweed (above), one of the first plants to regrow in the blast zone, brought color back to the area. The white blooms of avalanche lilies (left) were a welcome sight in the devastated blast zone.

Finally, in the summer of 1981, colors began to dot the gray land. First came the pink-flowered thistles and bright-red fireweed. Then, rain began to wash away the ash that was covering the roots of plants. As a result, many more plants were able to grow. Huckle-berries and thimbleberries sprouted. Blue lupine and white avalanche lilies bloomed. Green ferns grew on the roots of overturned trees.

Bugs and Birds Return

After the mountain erupted, scientists set special kinds of traps. The traps measured the amount of seeds that the wind blew into the blast zone. Spiders were also collected in the traps. Thousands of spiders arrived, carried by the wind on their long webs. The

Researchers check a trap for seeds and spiders.

spiders became food for the mountain bluebirds and northern flickers that had already returned to the area. The birds built their nests inside the splintered trees.

Some scientists working inside the mountain's crater wore colored safety suits that hummingbirds may have mistaken for flowers.

Hummingbirds, attracted by the fireweed flowers, soon flew into the blast zone. They even darted down at the scientists working in the volcano's crater. Perhaps they thought the scientists' colored safety suits were bright flowers.

Trees and Large Animals Return

Before Mount St. Helens erupted, the forest's trees were mostly evergreens, such as Douglas fir, hemlock, and Pacific silver fir. Some of these trees were more than three hundred years old.

After the wildflowers and bushes appeared, many trees

Tiny fir trees began to grow in the blast zone, but it will take hundreds of years for them to reach the size of the trees that were destroyed.

began to grow too. The first trees to grow were broadleaf trees, such as alder and cottonwood. Later, new evergreen trees began to grow in the blast zone.

Eventually, bear, deer, and elk began to wander back into the blast zone. Some of the elk gave birth to more calves than they usually do. It was nature's way of speeding up the renewal of the elk that were killed after the volcano's eruption.

Elk were among the first large animals to return to the blast zone.

Seeds collected in this elk track grew quickly because they didn't blow away.

As the big animals wandered through the blast zone, they left tracks in the ash. More windblown seeds collected in the tracks. When the seeds sprouted, the tracks became miniature flowerpots for the new plants.

Exploring the Monument

Each year since 1980, Mount St. Helens National Volcanic Monument looks different from the way it looked the year before. Every spring, more wildflowers bloom. The trees and bushes grow taller, and new seedlings sprout. Deer and elk wander through

A bear wanders through the newly growing trees and shrubs of the blast zone.

the blast zone. They feed on the tender branches of young trees. Once in a while, bears are seen eating huckleberries.

Scientists thought that it would take many years for life to return to the blast zone. But it has returned much more quickly than they expected. Today, you and your family can drive on a new highway to see this volcanic monument. The highway is about 50 miles (80 km) long. From two visitor centers near the highway's end, you can look across the avalanche and into the crater of Mount St. Helens.

Inside the crater, steam still rises from a mound of rock called a lava dome. The dome

The visitor centers offer spectacular views of the crater of Mount St. Helens (above). The lava dome inside the mountain's crater (left) began to form in 1980.

is made from molten (melted) rock. The rock cooled after oozing up into the crater from beneath the earth's surface. The lava dome formed after the main eruption in 1980. For years, the dome grew higher. It is now almost 1,000 feet (305 m) high.

From the visitor centers, rangers guide visitors along the trails. The rangers explain how nature is renewing the blast zone. You can also find

Rangers educate visitors about the monument (above). A worker plants seedlings to replace the trees that were destroyed in the eruption (left).

out what the scientists are learning. Other visitor centers along the new highway describe a different part of the story of Mount St. Helens.

One of the centers shows what a forest products company did after the volcano erupted. The company collected many of the fallen trees on its lands outside the monument. The trees were cut to make enough lumber to build 85,000 houses. Next, the company planted 18 million seedlings on 45,000 acres (18,211 ha) of land. The road to the monument takes visitors through this new forest.

There are other roads that lead to different areas of Mount St. Helens National Volcanic Monument. The monument also has more than 150 miles (241 km) of trails. If you hike through the monument, wear sturdy, comfortable shoes, carry water, and use sunscreen. Be sure to hike only on the marked trails. It is important that visitors do not disturb the plants and animals. That way, scientists can continue to learn

Visitors climb a sand-ladder trail (left) that keeps them from disturbing plants and animals. Signs (right) throughout the monument remind visitors to be careful of new plants.

how long it takes life to return to a blast zone after a volcano erupts. And you'll be helping other hikers to enjoy the beauty that you've seen!

To Find Out More

Here are some additional resources to help you learn more about Mount St. Helens National Volcanic Monument:

Carson, Rob. **The Living Mountain: Mount St. Helens.** Storytellers Ink, 1992.

Garlie, Gina. **Mount St. Helens Is My Home.** Lupine, 1993.

Hamilton, Sue. **Mount St. Helens Eruption.** Abdo & Daughters, 1989.

Taylor, Barbara. **Mountains & Volcanoes.** Kingfisher, 1993.

Cowlitz County Department of Tourism
207 Fourth Avenue North
Kelso, WA 98626

Forest Service United States Department of Agriculture
201 14th Street SW &
Independence Avenue SW
Washington, DC 20250

Mount St. Helens National Volcanic Monument
42218 NE Yale Bridge Road
Amboy, WA 98601

Earth's Active Volcanoes
http://www.geo.mtu.edu/volcanoes/world.html

Giant world map with active volcanoes numbered for quick reference and corresponding links to each site, including photos and information.

Great Outdoors Recreation Pages (GORP): Mount St. Helens National Volcanic Monument
http://www.gorp.com/gorp/resource/us_nm/main.html

Visit all of the national monuments, especially Mount St. Helens. You'll find history, photos, camping and fishing information, visitor centers, and schedules—plus links to hiking information at various monuments.

Mount St. Helens
http://www.teleport.com/~longview/msh.html

Learn about the blast, the devastation to human life, animals, vegetation, and property, and the regrowth that has followed. Great photos!

Mount St. Helens: Before and After
http://www.canby.com/~hemphill/helensa.html

Photos and stories from before, during, and after the great eruption.

Mount St. Helens National Volcanic Monument
http://vulcan.wr.usgs.gov/Msh/Living/PPF_MSH_monument.html

This U.S. Geological Survey site has maps, photos, history, and plenty of links to other sites.

Important Words

ash rock that is made into a powder when a volcano erupts

burrow hole or tunnel dug in the ground by an animal

crater hole in the ground made by an explosion

lava melted rock oozing from a volcano

national monument area set aside by the United States government for people to visit

renew to replace old or dead plants and animals with new ones

seedlings young trees that have been grown from seeds

Index

Meet the Authors

Sharlene and Ted Nelson were living 35 miles (56 km) from Mount St. Helens the day it erupted. They watched as the ash cloud rose into the sky, and as the mud flooded the rivers. Ted later assisted in the salvage of trees from part of the mountain's blast zone.

The Nelsons have written many articles about travel, as well as children's topics. Their most recent True Book title for Children's Press is *Olympic National Park.*

Photographs ©: Bob & Ira Spring: 9, 26 bottom, 43; Gary Braasch: cover, 12, 15, 17 bottom, 25 bottom, 29, 32, 38 top; Kirkendall-Spring Photographers: 38 bottom; Linda J. Moore: 40 top; Photo Researchers: 11 (Kraft Explorer/SS), 26 top (Tom & Pat Leeson), 25 top (John H. Meehan); Roger Werth: 20, 21; Tom & Pat Leeson: 2, 7, 23, 33, 36; U.S. Geological Survey, Vancouver, WA: 30; USDA Forest Service: 17 top (Gary Braasch), 34 (Jim Quiring); Weyerhaeuser Co.: 19, 40 inset.